A Glimpse of Love

by

Anjali Savalani

First paperback edition March 2024

Cover Photograph and Design by Shaunik Kalia

ISBN 979-8-8582-9273-9

anjalisavalani.com

*To the lovers, the dreamers,
and the believers...*

Immortal Love

We danced under the moonlight,
Just you and I,
The world was ours,
Only for the night.

We twirled 'neath the starry sky,
You held me close and tight,
Not wanting to let me go,
Not wanting me to disappear.

The music played for only two,
We danced like never before,
Cherishing our love,
With the time we had.

Our time to be together had ended;
You lived on Earth, I in Heaven,
And yet, it seemed as if,
We were always meant to be.

With tears in our hearts,
And love in our eyes,
Our lips met,
Warm against cold.

We hugged one last time,
One spirit, one being,
A mismatched, impossible pair,
Still, full of love.

In the end,
You looked at me,
I gazed back,
And our hands touched.

Not even death,
Could keep us apart,
Each time I vanished,
I returned to you again.

Another night, another day,
Time was running out for you,
Soon we would be together,
Forever and always.

<u>Shadows</u>

I have always been invisible,
Hiding behind curtains,
Away from the spotlight,
Never realizing when the folds began,
To embrace me into their world.

Being the center of attention,
Was never my intention;
When I was dragged to the light,
I ran to the shadows,
Getting caught in the darkness.

Then came one special day,
When a miracle took place,
An angel appeared before me,
He'd bring sunshine to my life,
A star in my everlasting night.

It surprised everyone to see,
One of their own turn away,
This was a miracle that didn't exist;
I soon learned a shadow,
Is never meant to be seen.

The angel was not who he claimed,
Not my savior, nor shining knight,
For he was but a human in disguise.
He saw me as the world did,
As nothing at all, invisible to his eyes.

He left me at the border,
The choice in my hands,
A step forward, I'd be welcomed,
Into their lives once and forever,
Or would I return to the shadows?

I have always been invisible,
Hidden behind curtains,
Safe and sound in the dark,
Why change now when,
There's no one waiting for me?

The answer was easy,
My way home was clear;
Those familiar were waiting,
Not whispering, but surely hoping,
That no angels would enter.

Step back. Step forward.
This hesitation lasted a minute,
But seeing the angel by the light,
Told me where I belonged,
Soon I was swallowed by the night.

I See You

For as long as I can remember,
The shadows have been
My one and only safe haven,
A place called home,
Where I am happy and free.

Out of sight, out of mind,
That's how it is,
And always would be,
Or so I thought,
Until it all changed forever.

I was done with angels,
And knights in shining armor,
No longer did that matter,
There were no saviors,
I'd saved myself from the world.

But then I saw you, all alone,
Standing close to the edge,
Near the shadows where I lived,
Which caught me by surprise,
Very rarely did people come here.

Curiosity got the best of me,
I am still human after all;
And the nearer I got,
It looked almost as if...
You were guarding the entrance?

Not for us shadows dwelling here,
But to all those people,
Who were straying too close,
You were there to help,
Turning them away from darkness.

As the days went by,
I watched your work,
And when you closed your eyes,
Laying down at the border,
Alone, unsafe and unaware.

The land of shadows would
Surely swallow you in soon,
I didn't know why I cared,
But I simply couldn't stand
To see that happen again.

I did what none other
Had ever dared to,
What no shadow could even
Claimed to have done,
I crossed over the border line.

There was light all around,
Bright, pure and blinding,
This world was not mine,
But there you slept,
And somehow I just knew.

As a shadow, I could
Remain unseen from you,
While still staying here,
To protect you as you
Did the same too.

I could make no sense,
Of what I'd just done,
Until you sat up, awake,
Looked right at me,
And said... *I see you.*

The Protector

In the world of shadows,
A rule unspoken exists,
Never does one cross over,
Towards the light outside,
Without losing the way back.

Yet I didn't think twice,
As I stepped forward,
Into the sunshine bright again,
To save one life,
Hoping to guard him close.

How long had it been,
Since I stood alone,
Away from all my darkness?
It didn't matter though,
When you suddenly said hello.

You see me as I am,
For there's a hand outstretched,
To move closer and away,
Past the boundaries behind,
Is it really that simple?

Who are you, why are you here?
All alone and with no fear;
Do these shadows not sway you?
Am I asking about the world,
Or the person in front of him?

What you say to me is simple,
"I must stay here and try,
To not let more shadows grow,
Surely that is worth the risk,
Being there for others in need?"

Now that I find myself,
In the light outside,
I can finally see the truth,
Therc is no need for knights
Or angels, when you are near.

This is a boy who is kind,
With no care for himself,
I reach for his hand,
He turns to the world,
But doesn't let go of me.

I may not have had someone
To stop me from falling,
And though I saved myself,
Even the protector of people,
Needs to be protected.

Who Are You?

I saw you standing there,
At the far side of the room,
Amidst the sea of faces I knew,
You were the one who stood out.
Who are you?

You saw me through all that crowd,
Your eyes gazed into mine,
I felt my heart stop,
I heard my breath catch,
This is different too.

Suddenly we're face to face,
Which one of us moved?
There's a smile in your eyes,
A light in your laughter
That echoes inside me.

There's a whole world around,
But I feel it's just you and me,
Do I know if you feel it?
You're a mystery, an unknown quantity,
And yet, so very safe.

It's the sound of your voice,
That gives me my first clue.
The touch of your hand on mine,
Tells me all I need to know,
Of course, it's really so simple.

"You're different than the others."
"What makes you so sure?"
I look around the room one last time,
The answer has been there all along,
"Because I know who you are."

You smile at me and lean forward,
A soft kiss on my cheek and a whisper,
"Then my work here is done."
I watch you walk away and disappear,
But there's only happiness in my heart.

"Hope."

<u>Tell Me...</u>

Tell me a story,
From years long past,
That shows that you
Trust me to keep
Secret from the world.

Tell me a secret,
Of things held dear
To your closed heart,
I'd keep them safe,
A memory for two.

Tell me a memory,
About the day when
Your dream came true,
I'll hold on tight,
Cherish it for you.

Tell me a dream,
Even small and simple,
Or big and difficult,
I am standing here...
Just tell me true.

<u>Happily Never After</u>

The first touch is unexpected,
But when our hands met,
It doesn't matter if there were
No sparks and no butterflies,
In that moment, it feels right.

The first hug is a surprise,
You make the first move,
Reaching towards him when
He needs to know that,
You are there for him.

The first date is perfectly imperfect,
A night filled with giggles,
Awkward pauses, hidden glances,
But the two of you are together,
You wouldn't change it for anything.

The first heartbreak is like glass,
Shattering into a thousand pieces
Yet still oh-so very silent.
This was no fairytale ending,
But perhaps it is a beginning?

<u>Love</u>

What do you think about,
When you talk of love?
The ones that last forever;
Be it from books, movies,
And yes, even on tv!

Do you imagine the story of
A man who would be king,
And the elven princess
Who chose her love over
Immortal life without a doubt?

Then there is the legend
About the madman and his
Blue police box, who burned
Up a sun to say goodbye
To his bad wolf girl.

One can also not forget
The son of a princess
And a scoundrel, who met
The scavenger from the desert,
Two halves of one soul.

And then you have us,
An ordinary girl and boy,
You're you and I'm me,
But maybe that is all
We really need to be?

Yin & Yang

The sun has the moon,
As I have you,
For all of the darkness,
There is light,
But which of us is which?

Every yin has its yang,
If you are white,
I must be black then;
Like a hero,
And the destined villain.

They say that opposites attract,
Is that really us?
Or are we rather more
The same being,
Two sides of one coin?

Where do you begin,
And I end?
What if there is nothing,
But an endless loop,
That links me and you?

A never-ending cycle of
Thinking that we,
Have saved each other,
When truth is,
We save ourselves together.

A Song of Fire & Ice

I was like fire,
And you were ice,
Two sides, one coin;
So why then, did
We crash and burn?

I was the yin,
To your yang, right?
They always tell you
That opposites do attract...
But nothing about destruction.

We could be described
As being two contrasts,
Still such mirrors, we,
I can't help wonder,
Where'd we go wrong?

Was it when my
Flames started to thaw
All of your ice?
And though I tried,
The fire burned brighter.

Or maybe your frost
That chilled my spark,
As you held me,
Which did start the
Beginning of our end?

Were we doomed to
Never be stable as
Two atoms that combine?
Looking around I see,
The explosion left behind.

Even if I'm light,
And you are dark,
First rays of dawn
Or last for dusk,
We're no longer... us.

<u>Forces of Nature</u>

There's lightning in your veins,
Thunder dancing along those fingers,
Dark eyes that mesmerize all,
Words sharp as a sword,
And cunning wit to match.

None would dare even try,
To stand up in defiance,
Against this mighty warrior,
Who is power incarnate,
The one they call protector.

But there is another around,
Who fights all with love,
A healer, but also fighter,
I am she who stands,
Between you and the world.

You who thinks the Earth,
Needs to be under control,
Can cast a thousand storms,
I will push them back,
My power is also tenfold.

Every snap, bite and crackle,
I meet with equal fierceness,
We're destined to fight,
For all of eternity, yes,
Yet it doesn't have to be so.

You are not a tempest,
To be tamed or leashed,
Surely there is another way,
For warrior and healer alike,
To end this enmity forever?

Years turn into decades now,
Soon it'll be centuries past,
Perhaps if we fought less,
We'd talk more, perhaps also
Find our way to peace?

There came a day when,
The warrior knelt before me,
With a crown of lightning,
*"Too long have we fought,
I am here to surrender."*

Those words echoed all around,
As the world waited to see;
I forsook claiming your power,
Instead, offered you my hand,
Two forces now become one.

The Ghost of You

When I look at you,
For one tiny second,
The world stops spinning,
And I find that
You are my anchor.

Just as sailors need
The North Star light,
Guiding them into the harbor,
So do I need you,
To lead me out from the night.

They say that every dusk,
Follows a new dawn,
Nights turn into days,
But when I'm with you,
Time stands still as stone.

Every second of every hour,
Be it day or night,
If we're always together,
Does it matter,
That you are not here?

Your whispers and your words,
Still belong to me,
In my heart and mind.
I love you,
Yes, the ghost of you.

To Love A Ghost

Have you ever wondered,
What it's like,
To love a ghost?
Caught in memories,
Of who you once,
Used to be?

With long curly hair,
Scuffed white sneakers,
And that disarming smile,
I still remember,
The way your voice,
Said my name.

The song that plays,
On the radio,
Reminds me of you;
I think about,
The last time we
Went dancing together.

Someone calls your name,
Whilst I'm shopping,
My head snaps up,
To see someone
Who isn't you, darling,
Of course not.

I walk past storefronts,
In their windows,
There stands a figure.
Could it be... no,
It's nothing more than
Lights playing tricks.

There's a familiar laughter,
Echoing all around,
And that lilt of
Your accent too,
Whispering in the air,
"I love you."

Every song and voice,
Face and smile,
All are you, but,
They're also not;
That is how you
Love a ghost.

<u>Chasing Ghosts</u>

I saw you standing under the sunlight,
As clear as a crystal shining bright,
The distance between us, a hundred feet,
Yet when you turned, our eyes did meet.

It's been years since we stood together,
In the same place at the same time,
Before I knew it, you stood before me,
Are you real? Or is this just...

I reached out a hand to touch,
As I laughed through these tears,
Your hand held mine close and tight,
This ghost is made flesh once more.

We defied the stars and also destiny,
Fought our way to the other side,
I've chased you across this universe;
Our time is finally here and now.

<u>The Rose</u>

A pink rose,
Offered as a gift,
From your hands to mine,
Tucked behind my ear,
Where it belongs.

A leather jacket,
Which fit you perfectly,
Like the one you wore,
That summer we met,
Five years ago.

A hand outstretched,
You stand there waiting,
For me to take hold,
I will follow you;
Into our tomorrow.

A promise unspoken,
Questions on my lips,
That no longer need asking,
I see your eyes,
Telling me everything.

A kiss shared,
Between two friends, lovers,
Who are now, at last
After all this time,
Finally together... forever.

What Is A Soulmate?

There is a legend of
The red string of fate,
An invisible thread that binds
Two souls together as one;
It is unbreakable and true.

Perhaps you have heard
The story of a twin flame,
A mirror to your soul,
They reveal the truth
Of who you really are.

And then there's the one
Who will guide you,
Whenever you are lost,
A compass bringing you home,
Your true North person.

They say that once,
We used to be one soul,
Split in half until we
Finally find each other again,
Soulmates reunited at long last.

You are not my first love,
I don't know about last,
But who's to say you aren't
My twin flame soulmate
Or even my North Star?

Is there a red string
That ties you to me?
Are you the other half
Of my incomplete soul?
I don't think I know.

It doesn't really matter
What name we give this,
There is no need to,
Why can't we just be
You and I, simply us?

Is this fate or destiny,
That's written in the stars?
We're two people who choose
To love and to be loved,
And that surely is enough.

I Close My Eyes

I close my eyes,
And I see you,
Not as you were,
But as you are,
Like you never left.

I close my eyes,
And I hear you,
With the same laugh,
That always made me
Smile from the heart.

I close my eyes
And I feel you,
Reaching for my hand,
You pull me in,
Safe in your arms.

I close my eyes,
And I know that
You will be there,
By my side until
The end of time.

I open my eyes,
And when I turn
To where I think
You are now standing,
What I see is...

<u>Here With You</u>

From stolen glances to lingered touches,
An unspoken secret,
We choose to keep for us,
Because needs must,
This love is special and new.

You twirl a lock of hair,
Pulling me near,
"When can we meet again?"
Is the question,
That you whisper against my ear.

Waiting by the stairs that night,
My heart skips,
When I see you standing there,
Making me wonder,
If you're thinking about me too.

We are dancing under the stars,
Hand in hand,
It feels like I could fly,
And only you,
Bring me back to solid ground.

This is what love feels like;
As if everything,
In the world finally makes sense,
Now that you,
Are here beside me at last.

Not-A-Date Date

It's not that I don't want
A typical date at all,
With flowers and chocolates,
Or a candlelit dinner perhaps,
Followed by a moonlit beach stroll.

Going to the movies sounds heavenly,
As does a picnic for two,
Playing video games together,
Or cuddling at home is romantic,
When it rains and storms outside.

But I want something else,
Still quite a cliché I suppose;
For you see, the only thing,
I could ever ask from you,
Is to just be there with me.

<u>Home Is Where The Heart Is</u>

The rain is a soft pitter-patter,
On our windowsill outside,
A fire crackles from within,
It's a quiet night for two.

We're working side by side,
Like two ships crossing paths,
But docked in one harbor,
Dinner is ready thanks to you.

I pour the wine with dessert,
Your hand seeks out mine,
And even doing the dishes
In perfect harmony is divine.

Tranquility

There's a silence all around,
Save for the ticking clock,
Counting down each second,
Every minute that passes by,
I breathe in and out.

You're working into the night,
As am I, beside you;
It's a quiet, calm peace,
The kind that comes from
Having been together since forever.

We don't need words or
Gestures to keep us going,
All it takes is one glance,
Or even a soft smile,
That speaks a thousand truths.

<u>I Know</u>

I know you love me,
In the little things
That you do or show,
Which mean as much
As the words ring true.

When you smile my way,
Laughing as you reach
For my hands to hold,
And when you wink,
It's like our little secret.

It's also when you leave
But always look back,
That's when I know.
Plus the silly emojis
You send about missing me.

Or when you rest your chin
On top of my head,
When you pull me close,
As we dance together
Even with no music playing.

From gentle caresses to the
Forehead kisses, every small
And big gesture is proof,
That you love me,
I know I do too.

Ask Me

Ask me to stay,
And I will,
Say that you're mine,
It is true,
Let the world know.

Ask me for love,
Here's my heart,
I'll hold onto yours,
Trust in us,
Nothing can change that.

Ask me what happens,
Come wind, storm,
Rain, and even snow,
I would say,
Sunshine will break through.

Ask me about anything,
I cannot lie,
Never to you love,
All I ask,
Is that you do.

Truth

Would I have loved you,
If things were different,
And our roles reversed?
Don't ask me because,
The truth is always yes.

Would I have loved you,
If perhaps we'd met,
In another time and place,
Strangers before we're friends?
I know that I would.

Would I have loved you,
If we never knew,
Each other at all somehow?
Reborn as someone else,
My soul would see yours.

Would I have loved you?
Is not the question,
Rather quite the opposite,
That I now must ask,
Do you love me?

Riddle, Mystery or Enigma?

For as long as I've known you,
There is only one thing
I can really say that I know,
You're like a riddle with no answer.

Is that even possible? I wonder and
Wonder some more to myself;
Maybe you're more akin to a mystery,
That needs to be unraveled?

I have questions and curiosities,
What makes you tick?
Who are you under all those layers,
Enigma with a name I cannot place?

One would ask, does it even matter?
Why do I even try,
To pull back that mask you wear,
And are surely hiding behind?

I would say that I- oh dear,
My mind's a slight blur,
Of course I know why, don't I?
.
.
.
.
.

"Why, it's love." You whisper.

The Key To His Heart

I used to think
You were this mystery,
Which needed a resolution,
But now I know
It's not about that.

You are everything and
Nothing all at once;
A master of secrets,
Who lives in shadow,
Hiding who you are.

If I could have
All of the answers,
It'd help me understand,
The heart of you,
Unmask the real man.

Your past defines you,
But it is not
All that you are,
I don't know everything,
Yet I know you.

My feelings never change,
This love is yours,
Nor do I ask,
For anything in return,
Or so I thought.

Never does anything stay
Hidden from an enigma,
Who knows all before
One can even speak,
It's a clever trick.
There came a day,

You held my hand,
And dropped a key,
Before I could ask...
.

.

.

.

.

"It opens my heart."

Pieces of A Puzzle

They say the greatest thing you'll ever learn,
Is just to love and be loved in return,
And it makes me wonder if I already have?

In the midst of chaos and madness,
One touch, one word, one look,
Drowns out the noise, there's only stillness.

Your laughter rings out across the room,
That smile, it makes my heart flutter,
Dark eyes searching for mine.

We've settled into a pattern of our own,
Like pieces of a puzzle that fit,
Imperfectly perfect together as we are.

<u>Riptide</u>

I fell in love with you,
The way one meets the sea,
Diving headfirst without even a thought.
It's only afterwards do I realize,
I don't know how to swim.

Loving you is exactly the same,
As if I'm caught in waves,
I start to wonder to myself,
Are you, darling, the ocean incarnate,
Or the island that is safety?

Everything about you is different than
Those that I have loved before,
It scares me, like I'm drowning;
Too fast, too soon, too much,
I have to resurface and breathe.

Are you pulling me back in?
No, I'm here on my own,
Knowing that to love you,
Means giving in to waters deep,
And hoping you'll hold me close.

"Don't let go," I think softly,
As I surrender to your embrace,
For if you do release me,
Then no rock, nor any shore,
Can anchor me to my salvation.

Awakened

I wish that I didn't
Feel the way I do,
But in spite of it
I really do love you,
With all of my heart.

There's a desire in me
Which I never had before,
Until you did awaken it
With but one touch dear,
Lighting a fire from within.

I want to share everything
With you, no holding back
It scares me to know,
I would bare my soul,
Truths, secrets and darkness too.

This need is much more
Than I can now stand
Let the dam burst open,
Will you be there standing,
To embrace all I am?

Our Once Upon A Time

If you had asked me,
When it was,
That you stole my heart?
I would say,
It began with a story.

What was first another morning,
Did suddenly change,
When a girl showed up,
Lost and scared,
She couldn't find her family.

There we were together dear,
In our bookshop,
A quiet day now abuzz
With this arrival,
We're all hands on deck.

You stayed with the child,
Sitting her down,
And you told her stories;
Of fierce princesses,
With their loyal dragon steeds.

A tale that had everything,
With friendship, bravery,
Sword fights and flights galore!
Her attention captured,
I sought to find help.

Yet before I strayed far,
The bell tinkled
As our doors then opened,
Mom and dad,
Had finally found us now.
Through the laughter and tears,

She was reunited,
With her parents at last,
The story ended,
As they all waved goodbye.

I suddenly felt it then,
That was when,
In the midst of panic,
You calmed me,
And I found my love.

<u>Safe Harbor</u>

A port in a storm,
You're my anchor,
One that keeps me grounded,
A dam holding
Every surge of the storm,
Well at bay.

When we're surrounded by chaos,
You're the calm,
An island full of safety,
Quelling rampaging tides,
Calming the deep, churning waters,
And all's well.

I could say so much
Of your strength,
But, before I can begin,
I suddenly find
A finger on my lips -
It's your turn.

"There's a force like none
That I've seen,"
You begin to say aloud,
"One beyond compare;
For trying to would simply
Not do justice."

"Strength, love and such kindness,
Compassion, trust, resolve;
These are but some words
To describe whom
I speak of - hardly all."
You reveal truthfully.

"She is but a human,
And yet somehow,
So much more than that.
What I try,
Is simply my very best,
To be there."

"As she is for me,
So shall I,
It's the least to do
For my love,
Don't you think so too?"
He asks me.

We're here for each other,
This I know,
But should the worst happen,
I'll be there,
To kiss away your tears,
As you, mine.

<u>Stages of Love</u>

First, it was your kindness
That I fell in love with,
The way you cared deeply,
Not just for me, but everyone
Whom you met; strangers even.

Whether a true, genuine smile,
Or thanks given for hard work,
And shaking hands with them,
Knowing names and faces aside,
Your positivity was pure and real.

Second after that, comes humor,
It's just as important I think;
I've found you have the gift,
To turn any frown around,
Chasing away the tears forever.

What follows next of course,
Is respect, dedication and loyalty.
These are all the qualities,
I see in you every day,
That you hold yourself to.

Last but not the least,
It was your heart, my beloved,
That you wore on your sleeve,
Which caught me off guard,
I wanted to save it.

More than that, I believe
You deserve all of the world,
With its joy and happiness,
Because behind every storm cloud,
There is always a rainbow.

<u>Anew</u>

The first drops of rain,
My last steps lie ahead;
I push through the door,
As I meet that downpour,
One chapter finished behind me.

Is it the beginning
Of the end? Or perhaps
A start of something new?
They say when a door closes,
Another one does open up.

Standing in the silence here,
I welcome these waters, yes,
Arms wide open and smiling,
Look! There's the sun shining,
Just hidden behind gray clouds.

Then I close my eyes,
While opening up my heart,
Should I dance a little,
Or jump in a puddle?
There's water all around now.

No questions or worries, doubts
And fears bother my mind,
For I know one truth,
The future is uncertain maybe,
But the present still beckons.

All About Love

Falling in love is like,
Missing the last step,
And finding you have slipped
Into a safe embrace,
Of an unexpected, real someone,
Who always catches you.

Your heart is akin to
A bird, that dives
Into a free fall blindly,
With no care for
Anything but just flying high,
By your lover's side.

The world is suddenly brighter,
Life feels sweeter too,
As the sayings always go;
Daylight is delightful joy,
And sleep brings me dreams
I welcome each night.

To simply hold your hand,
Or laugh with you,
That's all I ever need,
So stay here darling,
Let our love chase away,
All the shadows forever.

Little Things

It's about the little things,
Like the way you laugh,
When I say something,
The sound makes my heart
Stop right in its tracks.

Or when you muss up,
Your long dark hair,
Trying to flatten it down,
Hiding your eyes slightly,
And I forget to breathe.

It's the way you work,
With your sleeves rolled up,
Twirling a pen in hand,
And seeing that scrunched frown,
I promise not to giggle.

It's a glimmer of delight,
In those bright blue eyes,
When the answer finds you,
I see it reflected within,
I'm all ears to listen.

It's the way your voice,
Carries itself to rest,
In my ears and heart,
The sound makes me stumble;
I feel like I'm dreaming.

And when I turn around,
To see you standing there,
I reach for your hand,
To steady me on my feet,
Only to touch thin air.

<u>In Memory, Darling</u>

You had asked me once,
If the chips were down,
And it came to this;
Would I give my soul
To the Devil, for you?

I didn't have the answer,
Not then anyway, for reasons
I dared not reveal aloud,
But now, standing here today,
To you, I do say...

If I had one wish,
All I would want is,
For you to not forget;
Even if I'm not yours,
As you are not mine.

I'll ask you to think,
Of the days we had,
Too little though they were,
They're all that is left,
Keep me in your memories.

When you walk down streets,
Seeing the world pass by,
Know you are not alone,
For you'll feel my hand,
Always there at your side.

When you close your eyes,
Every once in a while,
The only thing I ask,
Is to simply let yourself,
Just dream about me maybe.

As long as you remember,
As long as you live,
I'd give my soul away,
Because darling, no matter what,
You'll always have my heart.

Matching Pieces

Would you still love me,
If the truth was laid bare,
That under every single layer,
Hides one simple, true fact,
I am not whole anymore?

Would you still love me,
Pieces and all? I'm not
Who the world sees outside,
There are cracks in this armor,
My heart still hasn't healed.

Would you still love me,
Knowing about the missing pieces?
I am incomplete; not more
Than a shadow now alas,
With no tether, no sanctuary?

Before I can say anything else,
Your finger is on my lips,
And you ask to speak,
Saying these questions do indeed
Have an answer for me.

"I love you for you,
With all your sharp edges,
Missing parts, cracks and tears,
It makes me love you more,
Not less; nothing will change that."

"We're all a little broken darling,
But maybe you and I could
See where this journey takes us,
And find our happily ever after,
Somewhere along the way?"

<u>What Is Love?</u>

Love is standing in the rain,
Under an umbrella,
And offering shelter to one,
Who forgot theirs,
In a haste that morning.

Love is listening to your sibling,
When they cry,
Giving them a shoulder too,
As they have,
When you had needed one.

Love is hiding under the blankets,
Smiling to yourself,
Texting your cute partner from class,
Then falling asleep,
Under the moonlit, starry sky.

Love is holding out a hand,
To be greeted,
By a little furry friend,
Who was alone,
Until he finds his new home.

Love is hugging both parents,
After day's end,
Hard work is always rewarded,
With warm meals,
And a place to rest.

Love is about saying yes,
To yourself first,
Before anyone else in life,
Choose your happiness,
Be captain of team you.

Love is waking up to sunshine,
Not from outside,
But the smile by your side,
Holding your hand,
Since you both said, *"I do."*

Love is a bundle of joy,
Whom you cherish,
Seeing them crawl and walk,
Soon, even running,
Back home to you.

So when someone asks you,
What love is,
You can tell them this -
It is everything,
That you say it is.

<u>Ours</u>

You once asked me for a story,
To share between the two of us,
A wish that caught me by surprise;
Because it was more than just that,
You wanted to hear something true.

So I sat down beside you and
Began talking about a tale of love,
Of polaric destiny as it were -
There was a dreamer of a girl,
Who fell for an impossible boy.

Two opposites that did not attract,
Because they were too unlike the other.
No matter what they each tried,
She loved too much and too deeply,
But he cared naught for feelings.

A pair so mismatched, that even angels
Would fall in love with demons;
They'd still make more sense together.
You might even say the sun
And the moon would work well too.

"I don't think I like this story,"
You started to say just then,
*"It sounds too made up to be true,
Even the most unlikely of people
Can find their way to each other."*

I smiled at you and said,
*"You asked me for the truth,
This is what I had to give."*
You glanced my way and wondered,
"Well yes, but whose truth is it?"

Of all the clues in the story,
Which there aren't very many,
I simply chose to walk away instead,
Letting the wind carry my answer,
As I whispered softly to you, *"Ours."*

Tattoos

Your body is a canvas,
And ink, the paint
Used to tell a story,
Of this life anew,
Each one unique to you.

There, on your left arm,
A tattoo that heralds
What you once described as
The dawn of hope,
That's always still in bloom.

Across your right wrist now,
I see those lyrics,
To the song you hum,
Then so do I,
Which forever makes me smile.

Let's not forget the ribbon
Of infinity, a bond
Forged during the good times
And even the bad,
Two sides of true friendship.

Last but surely not least,
Is the special one,
That's held dearly to you,
Your words not mine,
For what saved your life.

And then you asked me,
Out of the blue,
If I could have one,
What would I choose,
For my very own tattoo?

My skin may be bare,
But I already know,
If you could look within,
Your name is etched,
In my heart and soul.

<u>Rewind</u>

I think about the day we met,
Of how things first went,
What did we say and even do?
All these years later now,
The time we spent has blurred together.

It was a rocky and uneven start,
Filled with many awkward fumbles,
Tripping over my words a little,
Thankfully not over my feet,
Save that one time you caught me.

The years went by like a breeze,
With days of laughs and smiles,
Yet also of quiet wonderings too,
Filled with longing stares, daydreams...
Too late I realized, I fell in love.

Here we are after things have settled,
You and I found balance,
A comfortable ease like never before,
Still, I wonder to myself,
About the path that wasn't taken.

Would things be any different,
If day one was changed?
I could go back and do it over,
Say this to you, not that,
Be more of who I am today.

Yes, that's just what we need,
You are a friend indeed,
But what if we could be more?
Let me grab time's remote,
And hit rewind to the beginning.

The Thief

Quiet as a hidden shadow,
I am there but not,
Always on the edge watching,
Waiting for my only chance,
When I can step within.

"Don't ever get too close,"
The voices say to me,
I know I cannot linger,
But there is one treasure,
That pulls me in deeper.

You opened the door wide,
Saw through into my soul,
Listened to all I spoke,
With a hand to hold,
Yet you kept yourself closed.

"Turn away, quickly now dear,"
They warned this clever girl,
I never learned to listen,
And when I dared myself,
The answers always did follow.

There was another I discovered,
Who had your true self.
All I was left with,
My name on your lips,
But never like a prayer.

"What is left to do?"
Take the pieces of you;
My crime was to love,
I may be a thief,
But you stole my heart.

The Last Wish

When the clock strikes 11:11,
I close my eyes and think,
If I could have a wish,
It would be simply this,
To see you one last time.

I'd take the genie's lamp,
With a magic carpet ride,
Cross oceans far and wide,
Holding hope in my heart,
That you'll be waiting there.

I'll watch a shooting star fall,
Say the rhyme out loud,
Blow on a dandelion even,
To make my dream come true,
It's time I said *"I love you."*

Masquerade

If this world's a stage,
And we are mere actors,
Then surely it must mean,
The roles decided for us,
Are all we may play?

There's a time and place,
For each act, each scene,
Our lines have been written,
The curtains start to rise,
As we don our masks.

We are children and siblings,
Friends and lovers in life,
One day parents and grandparents,
But who are we really,
Within all these different identities?

Standing in front of me,
Holding out your hand now,
It's time for the denouement,
You and I must part,
There is no happy ending.

"But what if there was?"
Let's go against it all,
Cast off these shackles darling,
Throw caution to the wind,
This is our story's beginning.

Love At 12:18 pm

I remember like it was yesterday,
When I realized how I felt,
I will say naught but truth,
One summer's day back in June,
The clock at quarter past noon.

The sun started to shine bright,
And just like in the movies,
I glanced up to see you,
With that quiet smile lighting up,
Is there a halo around too?

It was a soft comforting hug,
The way you settled in surely,
Finding a home in my heart,
You looked at me just then,
And that was when I knew.

In This World

The sun had already start to sct,
As we walked home together,
Shoulders bumping now and then,
Hands almost, but not yet touching,
The world is quiet all around us.

I turn my gaze towards you,
Bathed in the glow of sunlight,
Your eyes already on mine,
All I've never said waits patiently,
It's time I voice everything aloud.

A raised eyebrow in silent question,
You ask me if I'm alright,
For a moment I imagine it,
Saying those three words aloud,
How would it turn out in the end?

There's a universe to the left of this,
And I wonder about us there,
Did we take a chance on love?
See where it would lead to,
Is the world brighter there perhaps?

But here and now in our world,
Standing side by side together,
Everything feels a million miles away,
My heart is bleeding as I say,
"Please, can I ask you to stay?"

Eternal

You came into my life
Like a bolt of lightning,
Striking when I didn't expect,
Didn't plan on meeting you,
And you stayed with me.

It started slow at first,
The way you broke through,
Knocking down all my walls,
Settling within these very veins,
Opening my heart to trust.

But you went deeper still,
Reaching where my soul lay,
No longer was it alone;
This was the other half,
I never knew I'd lost.

How can I even think,
Of this world without you,
Our lives are one now,
Darling can we be together,
Until the end of forever?

A Tale For Two

I have a dream,
Where I take your vision,
Turn it into reality,
Lights, camera, action!
The stage is set for our story.

It's a tale of love,
With all the right beats;
Two friends, now something more,
Working together to solve
The world's greatest mystery.

Across oceans and deserts,
We're on a long journey,
To find one simple truth,
What does it mean,
When you say you're in love?

Through thick and thin,
In all corners of the Earth,
It's just the two of us,
Shall we say, partners-in-crime,
Or almost, not quite... right?

There's a stumble, slight trouble,
But when I do fall,
You've caught me surely,
Keeping me safe and sound,
Listen closely, it's the climax now.

There's no dragons to fight,
Still, it's an epic we write,
One last flourish is left,
Let's make it our best,
Before the curtain comes down.
Shall we end this,

The way they always do?
With a happily ever after
For me and for you,
But we're not in a movie.

<u>Return Home</u>

There's a whisper in the wind,
Of a life already lived,
Are all my dreams really dreams,
Or perhaps they are memories,
When I lived amongst the stars...

I had the moon for company,
And on those sleepless nights,
We'd talk all through the night,
A friend who would listen,
Never judging, yet always beside me.

Each day the sun shone bright,
Marking a new day's beginning,
But I could feel something missing,
I longed for real adventure,
To explore the world down below.

So then I closed my eyes,
With one bag in hand,
Made a wish upon a star,
To be where the humans are,
A mortal life now called out.

It was more than my imagination,
Could even begin to fathom,
I had a family and friends,
A place where I belonged,
And soon, I found someone special.

But truth came to me unbidden
There was a choice given,
Stay and forget my old life,
Or leave and lose everything,
I am, after all, not human.

What makes this life worth living,
If not each other's souls?
And these hearts that connect us,
Hands who lift us up,
When we fall and also stumble.

To be here is a gift,
One I do truly cherish,
I love and I am loved,
There is but one choice,
As I hold on to you.

Marry Me Chicken

There's a recipe online,
'Marry Me Chicken' it says,
Along with the story,
Of proposals that soon follow,
To me it seems,
Too good to be true.

It gives me pause,
Surely this isn't real?
Yet I find myself,
Thinking about a what if?
Which is followed by,
What would you do?

Let's say I cook,
This special marry me chicken,
Would it lead you,
To just say the words?
Which later turn into,
"For better or worse, I do."

Or maybe something slower,
That starts with the dishes,
Would you take over,
And after if there's time,
We then dance together,
With a glass of wine?

Would you wait until
The clock chimes at midnight?
Finding the perfect moment,
To go with chocolate mousse,
How will you say,
"Would you be mine forever?"

Maybe it doesn't matter
If it's one or the other,
I must decide to
Take a chance at first,
But wait, oh dear...
I'm all out of chicken.

Acknowledgements

I've been writing poems since I was 16, and I never really imagined myself getting to a point in my life where I saw them reaching the entire world once they were published. I'm sure everyone knows just how deeply personal and close to one's heart poems tend to be. Over the years, I had a lot of people who always told me that these were worth sharing with the rest of you all, and it's thanks to their constant support, encouragement and a shared enthusiasm that I made the leap to becoming a published poet!

It was a group effort to get here; writing may be seen as a lonely profession, but with the right people by your side who cheer you on through the good times and the bad, the highs and the lows, when you have someone who believes in you, then anything is possible! It takes a village, as the saying goes, and it's because of my village that I am where I am today. So without further ado, these next few pages are dedicated to my friends and family who have been a part of this journey with me, staying by my side until the finish line!

As a writer, I've always said that if my words can reach even one person, that is just as important as reaching dozens! So before anyone else, my first thanks is to you, reader, who has picked up this book and arrived here at the end. Everything that I write is for you; I hope that whatever reason you picked up this book to read was fulfilled, and even if not, then perhaps it at least offered a momentary escape to a world full of love in all its many aspects - happiness and sadness, giddiness and heartbreak, joy and angst, two sides of the same coin!

Next, I'd like to say thank you to Richa, my
self-appointed manager, editor, marketing director,
cheerleader, no. 1 supporter and my best friend.
Without you, none of this would have been
possible. It's because you are an amazing person
that I was able to make this dream into a reality!
From all the late night talks to the endless emails,
helping me iron out each and every detail, our hard
work has finally come to fruition in the form of this
book!

A double thanks goes to Sakhi and Shabeena,
my two best friends who have been on this journey
with me since day zero - when these were just
poems that were written and posted on a private
blog, when there was no sign of an actual book,
when all I had were two readers and two emotional
support besties; we started with the three of us and
look at how far we've finally come after all these
years!

Thank you Sammy, who is the reason these poems
are out there in the big wide world; for every push
and nudge that you gave me, merely saying thanks
isn't enough. For being there to listen and also
write with me and share in this amazing journey
that we've been through for so many years now!
For all of the writing exercises, which were a gift
and a blessing. For being my partner-in-crime and
co-writer extraordinaire.

I also have to say thank you to Shaunik, one of my
dearest and oldest friends, for your absolutely
breathtaking photography skills that gave me this
beautiful cover - it was the missing piece that I
didn't even know I was looking for, but when I
found it, I knew that my book would be incomplete
without it. Not to mention your impeccable editing
that resulted in the perfect design as well!

Thanks to Antonio, my friend and mentor, for giving me the motivation I needed at almost every writer's block that I encountered; through countless texts that spanned not just days or weeks, but months of nitpicks and worries, you helped me with it all. You encouraged me to never give up on my dreams, showed me how to believe in myself when I needed it; and whether it was your witty one-word advice or the more detailed words of wisdom, both were equally important to me.

I can't forget my second mentor as well, Kevin! You are as wise as you are kind; your friendship is a gift and having known you for the last three years has taught me so much; your opinion always matters! The famous saying, "actions speak louder than words" has never been truer than your support and guidance, which helped me to navigate this entire experience. Thank you for everything.

And last but not the least, thank you to my family - my mom, my brother, my sister-in-law, all of my cousins, aunts and uncles, nieces and nephews and everyone in between! I'm officially an author now!